HEART, MIGHT, MIND

& STRENGTH

A JOURNAL FOR SISTER MISSIONARIES

CFI • CEDAR FORT PUBLISHING, INC.
SPRINGVILLE, UTAH

ISBN 13: 978-1-4621-1710-9

Published by CFI, an imprint of Cedar Fort, Inc.
2373 W. 700 S., Springville, UT 84663
Distributed by Cedar Fort, Inc., www.cedarfort.com

LIBRARY OF CONGRESS CONTROL NUMBER: 2015935357

Page design by Teresa Collins
Cover design by Lauren Error
Cover design © 2015 by Lyle Mortimer
Edited by Eileen Leavitt

Printed in China

10 9 8 7 6 5 4 3 2 1

Printed on acid-free paper

SHALL I FALTER OR SHALL I

finish

THOMAS S. MONSON

S M T W T F S

S M T W T F S

JOURNAL

S M T W T F S

MONTH   DAY   YEAR

YOU ARE NOT *called* TO SERVE IN A PLACE.
YOU ARE CALLED TO
SERVE IN PLACE OF THE *savior*

AREA: _____

TRANSFER IN DATE: _____   TRANSFER OUT DATE: _____

COMPANION(S): _____

_____

HIGHLIGHTS: _____

_____

_____

_____

_____

_____

_____

_____

_____

_____

_____

_____

_____

_____

_____

_____

_____

_____

AREA: _____

TRANSFER IN DATE: _____ TRANSFER OUT DATE: _____

COMPANION(S): _____

_____

HIGHLIGHTS: _____

_____

_____

_____

_____

_____

_____

_____

_____

_____

_____

_____

_____

_____

_____

_____

_____

_____

MY AREA

AREA: _____

TRANSFER IN DATE: _____   TRANSFER OUT DATE: _____

COMPANION(S): _____

_____

HIGHLIGHTS: _____

_____

_____

_____

_____

_____

_____

_____

_____

_____

_____

_____

_____

_____

_____

_____

_____

_____

MY AREA

AREA: _____

TRANSFER IN DATE: _____ TRANSFER OUT DATE: _____

COMPANION(S): _____

_____

HIGHLIGHTS: _____

_____

_____

_____

_____

_____

_____

_____

_____

_____

_____

_____

_____

_____

_____

_____

_____

_____

_____

AREA: _____

TRANSFER IN DATE: _____   TRANSFER OUT DATE: _____

COMPANION(S): _____

_____

HIGHLIGHTS: _____

_____

_____

_____

_____

_____

_____

_____

_____

_____

_____

_____

_____

_____

_____

_____

_____

_____

MY AREA

AREA: _____

TRANSFER IN DATE: _____ TRANSFER OUT DATE: _____

COMPANION(S): _____

_____

HIGHLIGHTS: _____

_____

_____

_____

_____

_____

_____

_____

_____

_____

_____

_____

_____

_____

_____

_____

_____

_____

_____

_____

MY AREA

AREA: _____

TRANSFER IN DATE: _____   TRANSFER OUT DATE: _____

COMPANION(S): _____

_____

HIGHLIGHTS: _____

_____

_____

_____

_____

_____

_____

_____

_____

_____

_____

_____

_____

_____

_____

_____

_____

_____

MY AREA

AREA: _____

TRANSFER IN DATE: _____ TRANSFER OUT DATE: _____

COMPANION(S): _____

_____

HIGHLIGHTS: _____

_____

_____

_____

_____

_____

_____

_____

_____

_____

_____

_____

_____

_____

_____

_____

_____

_____

_____

MY AREA

AREA: _____

TRANSFER IN DATE: _____   TRANSFER OUT DATE: _____

COMPANION(S): _____

_____

HIGHLIGHTS: _____

_____

_____

_____

_____

_____

_____

_____

_____

_____

_____

_____

_____

_____

_____

_____

_____

_____

MY AREA

AREA: _____

TRANSFER IN DATE: _____ TRANSFER OUT DATE: _____

COMPANION(S): _____

_____

HIGHLIGHTS: _____

_____

_____

_____

_____

_____

_____

_____

_____

_____

_____

_____

_____

_____

_____

_____

AREA: _____

TRANSFER IN DATE: _____   TRANSFER OUT DATE: _____

COMPANION(S): _____

_____

HIGHLIGHTS: _____

_____

_____

_____

_____

_____

_____

_____

_____

_____

_____

_____

_____

_____

_____

_____

_____

THESE ARE YOUR
DAYS TO STAND *Strong*

AS DISCIPLES OF THE LORD JESUS CHRIST

NEIL L. ANDERSEN

MIRACLES

TODAY'S MIRACLE

DATE: /   /

MIRACLES

TODAY'S MIRACLE

DATE: /   /

TODAY'S MIRACLE

DATE: / /

TODAY'S MIRACLE

TODAY'S MIRACLE

DATE: /   /

TODAY'S MIRACLE   DATE: /   /

TODAY'S MIRACLE

DATE: /   /

TODAY'S MIRACLE

DATE: / /

TODAY'S MIRACLE

MIRACLES

TODAY'S MIRACLE

DATE: / /

TODAY'S MIRACLE

DATE: / /

TODAY'S MIRACLE

TODAY'S MIRACLE

DATE: /   /

TODAY'S MIRACLE

DATE: /   /

MIRACLES

TODAY'S MIRACLE

DATE: /   /

TODAY'S MIRACLE

DATE: /   /

ASAP

ALWAYS STOP AND PRAY

INSPIRATION

SCRIPTURE INSPIRATION

BOOK

CHAPTER

VERSE(S)

THOUGHTS . . .

SCRIPTURE INSPIRATION

BOOK

CHAPTER

VERSE(S)

THOUGHTS . . .

SCRIPTURE INSPIRATION

BOOK

CHAPTER

VERSE(S)

THOUGHTS . . .

SCRIPTURE INSPIRATION

BOOK

CHAPTER

VERSE(S)

THOUGHTS . . .

SCRIPTURE INSPIRATION

BOOK

CHAPTER

VERSE(S)

THOUGHTS . . .

SCRIPTURE INSPIRATION

BOOK

CHAPTER

VERSE(S)

THOUGHTS . . .

SCRIPTURE INSPIRATION

BOOK

CHAPTER

VERSE(S)

THOUGHTS . . .

SCRIPTURE INSPIRATION

BOOK

CHAPTER

VERSE(S)

THOUGHTS . . .

INSPIRATION

SCRIPTURE INSPIRATION

BOOK

CHAPTER

VERSE(S)

THOUGHTS . . .

SCRIPTURE INSPIRATION

BOOK

CHAPTER

VERSE(S)

THOUGHTS . . .

SCRIPTURE INSPIRATION

BOOK	
CHAPTER	
VERSE(S)	

THOUGHTS . . .

SCRIPTURE INSPIRATION

BOOK

CHAPTER

VERSE(S)

THOUGHTS . . .

SCRIPTURE INSPIRATION

BOOK	
CHAPTER	
VERSE(S)	

THOUGHTS . . .

SCRIPTURE INSPIRATION

BOOK

CHAPTER

VERSE(S)

THOUGHTS . . .

SCRIPTURE INSPIRATION

BOOK

CHAPTER

VERSE(S)

THOUGHTS . . .

SCRIPTURE INSPIRATION

BOOK

CHAPTER

VERSE(S)

THOUGHTS . . .

INSPIRATION

SCRIPTURE INSPIRATION

BOOK

CHAPTER

VERSE(S)

THOUGHTS . . .

SCRIPTURE INSPIRATION

BOOK

CHAPTER

VERSE(S)

THOUGHTS . . .

SCRIPTURE INSPIRATION

BOOK

CHAPTER

VERSE(S)

THOUGHTS . . .

SCRIPTURE INSPIRATION

BOOK

CHAPTER

VERSE(S)

THOUGHTS . . .

S C R I P T U R E   I N S P I R A T I O N

BOOK

CHAPTER

VERSE(S)

ASK, AND IT SHALL BE

given

SEEK, AND YE SHALL *find*

MATTHEW 7:7

CONFERENCE

CONFERENCE

THERE ARE LIVES TO *brighten*

THERE ARE *hearts* TO TOUCH

THERE ARE *souls* TO SAVE

THOMAS S. MONSON

NAME:

HOW WE MET:

DATE:

LOCATION:

STORY:

CONTACT INFO:

NAME:

HOW WE MET:

DATE:

LOCATION:

STORY:

CONTACT INFO:

NAME:

HOW WE MET:

DATE:

LOCATION:

STORY:

CONTACT INFO:

NAME:

HOW WE MET:

DATE:

LOCATION:

STORY:

CONTACT INFO:

NAME:

HOW WE MET:

DATE:

LOCATION:

STORY:

CONTACT INFO:

NAME:

HOW WE MET:

DATE:

LOCATION:

STORY:

CONTACT INFO:

NAME:

HOW WE MET:

DATE:

LOCATION:

STORY:

CONTACT INFO:

NAME:

HOW WE MET:

DATE:

LOCATION:

STORY:

CONTACT INFO:

NAME:

HOW WE MET:

DATE:

LOCATION:

STORY:

CONTACT INFO:

NAME:

HOW WE MET:

DATE:

LOCATION:

STORY:

CONTACT INFO:

CONTACTS

NAME:

HOW WE MET:

DATE:

LOCATION:

STORY:

CONTACT INFO:

NAME:

HOW WE MET:

DATE:

LOCATION:

STORY:

CONTACT INFO:

NAME:

HOW WE MET:

DATE:

LOCATION:

STORY:

CONTACT INFO:

NAME:

HOW WE MET:

DATE:

LOCATION:

STORY:

CONTACT INFO:

NAME:

HOW WE MET:

DATE:

LOCATION:

STORY:

CONTACT INFO:

NAME:

HOW WE MET:

DATE:

LOCATION:

STORY:

CONTACT INFO:

NAME:

HOW WE MET:

DATE:

LOCATION:

STORY:

CONTACT INFO:

NAME:

HOW WE MET:

DATE:

LOCATION:

STORY:

CONTACT INFO:

NAME:

HOW WE MET:

DATE:

LOCATION:

STORY:

CONTACT INFO:

NAME:

HOW WE MET:

DATE:

LOCATION:

STORY:

CONTACT INFO:

NAME:

HOW WE MET:

DATE:

LOCATION:

STORY:

CONTACT INFO:

SOMETIMES A SINGLE
PHRASE OF TESTIMONY
CAN SET EVENTS IN MOTION
THAT AFFECT SOMEONE'S LIFE FOR

eternity

DIETER F. UCHTDORF

S M T W T F S

TESTIMONY

DATE: _____

TESTIMONY

TESTIMONY

TESTIMONY

TESTIMONY

S M T W T F S

DATE: _____

TESTIMONY

EVERY DAY MAY NOT BE *good* BUT THERE IS SOMETHING GOOD IN EVERY DAY

DATE TAKEN:_____ PLACE:_____

STORY:_____

_____

_____

_____

_____

_____

_____

DATE TAKEN:_____   PLACE:_____

STORY:_____

_____

_____

_____

_____

_____

_____

DATE TAKEN:_____ PLACE:_____

STORY:_____

_____

_____

_____

_____

_____

_____

DATE TAKEN:_____   PLACE:_____

STORY:_____

_____

_____

_____

_____

_____

_____

DATE TAKEN:_____ PLACE:_____

STORY:_____

_____

_____

_____

_____

_____

_____

DATE TAKEN:_____   PLACE:_____

STORY:_____

_____

_____

_____

_____

_____

_____

DATE TAKEN:_____ PLACE:_____

STORY:_____

_____

_____

_____

_____

_____

_____

DATE TAKEN:_____ PLACE:_____

STORY:_____

_____

_____

_____

_____

_____

_____

DATE TAKEN:_____ PLACE:_____

STORY:_____

_____

_____

_____

_____

_____

_____

DATE TAKEN:_____   PLACE:_____

STORY:_____

_____

_____

_____

_____

_____

_____

DATE TAKEN:_____ PLACE:_____

STORY:_____

_____

_____

_____

_____

_____

_____

DATE TAKEN:_____ PLACE:_____

STORY:_____

_____

_____

_____

_____

_____

_____

_____

DATE TAKEN:_____ PLACE:_____

STORY:_____

_____

_____

_____

_____

_____

_____

PICTURES

DATE TAKEN:_____   PLACE:_____

STORY:_____

_____

_____

_____

_____

_____

_____

DATE TAKEN:_____ PLACE:_____

STORY:_____

_____

_____

_____

_____

_____

_____

DATE TAKEN:_____   PLACE:_____

STORY:_____

_____

_____

_____

_____

_____

_____

DATE TAKEN:_____ PLACE:_____

STORY:_____

_____

_____

_____

_____

_____

_____

_____

IT IS IMPOSSIBLE FOR US
TO FAIL WHEN WE DO OUR

best

WHEN WE ARE ON THE
LORD'S ERRAND

M. RUSSELL BALLARD

STORIES FROM THE DAY

NAME:

DATE:

PLACE:

STORIES FROM THE DAY

NAME:

DATE:

PLACE:

STORIES FROM THE DAY

NAME:

DATE:

PLACE:

STORIES FROM THE DAY

STORIES FROM THE DAY

NAME:

DATE:

PLACE:

STORIES FROM THE DAY

NAME:

DATE:

PLACE:

STORIES FROM THE DAY

NAME:

DATE:

PLACE:

STORIES FROM THE DAY

NOTES

Thomas S. Monson, "I Will not Fail Thee, nor Forsake Thee," *Ensign*, November 2013.

Neil L. Andersen, "Spiritual Whirlwinds," *Ensign*, April 2014.

Matthew 7:7

Thomas S. Monson, "True Shepherds," *Ensign*, November 2013.

Dieter F. Uchtdorf, "Waiting on the Road to Damascus," *Ensign*, May 2011.

M. Russell Ballard, "Put Your Trust in the Lord," *Ensign*, November 2013.